20% House

THE ANGER IN ERNEST AND ERNESTINE

ROBERT MORGAN   MARTHA ROSS   LEAH CHERNIAK

Playwrights Canada Press
Toronto

The Anger in Ernest and Ernestine
Copyright © 1987 Robert Morgan, Martha Ross, Leah Cherniak

PLAYWRIGHTS CANADA PRESS is the imprint of
PLAYWRIGHTS UNION OF CANADA
54 Wolseley Street, 2nd Floor
Toronto, Ontario, Canada M5T 1A5
Phone (416) 947–0201

PLAYWRIGHTS UNION OF CANADA operates with generous assistance from the Canada Council, the Department of External Affairs, the Ontario Ministry of Culture and Communications, the Ontario Arts Council, Alberta Culture, Alberta Foundation for the Literary Arts, the Municipality of Metropolitan Toronto—Cultural Affairs Division, and the City of Toronto through the Toronto Arts Council.

Front cover photo by Amir Gavriely.
Front cover design by Tony Hamill.
Editor: Tony Hamill.

Canadian Cataloguing in Publication Data
Morgan, Robert, 1950-
     The anger in Ernest and Ernestine

A play.
ISBN 0–88754–492–4

I. Cherniak, Leah, 1956- . II. Ross, Martha, 1954- . III. Title.

PS8576.O74A8 1990   C812'.54   C90–093131-0
PR9199.3.M67A8 1990

First Edition: July 1990
Printed and bound in Canada.

THE ANGER IN
ERNEST AND ERNESTINE

We dedicate this publication to Susan Morgan because of her support, her wisdom and her love.

The Anger in Ernest and Ernestine premiered in a Theatre Columbus production at the Poor Alex Theatre, Toronto in May, 1987. It was subsequently performed at the Kaasa Theatre, Edmonton, sponsored by the Northern Light Company. The cast for both productions was:

ERNEST   *Robert Morgan*
ERNESTINE   *Martha Ross*

Directed by Leah Cherniak.
Set design by Shaun Lynch.
Lighting design by Glenn Davidson.

All songs and music in this play were composed by George Axon with vocals by Mag Ruffman and Robert Morgan. The incidental music is marked in the stage directions and each piece has been given a title.

The Anger in Ernest and Ernestine was the winner of the 1988 Dora Mavor Moore Award for Best Production in the Small Theatre Category and garnered five other nominations.

The authors would like to acknowledge the support of the Canada Council, The Ontario Arts Council, The Ministry of Culture and Communications and the Toronto Arts Council and would like to thank the following people for their assistance and support at various times during this project: Glenn Davidson, Eric Rice, Jennifer Brewin, Luisa Trisi, Julie Bishop, Factory Theatre, Deb Porter, Amir Gavriely.

Special thanks to Kelley Nadal, Gwen Baillie and Philip Nessel for their contributions to the show, particularly for transcribing the tapes and formulating the stage directions.

A NOTE FROM THE AUTHORS

The Anger in Ernest and Ernestine is, in every sense, a collaboration. It was a heated, late-night discussion that first lead us to our theme. Our first step was to research written material on the topic of anger but what was far more inspirational was reflecting on personal experiences...our own and those of others. It seemed that everyone we talked to suddenly became animated when we described our ideas for exploring anger in long-term relationships. As if to cheer us on, many took the opportunity to tell us, often in vivid detail, previously undisclosed personal anecdotes. We would find ourselves howling with laughter at the most excruciatingly painful things. We knew we were on to something.

The characters, Ernestine and Ernest, were developed through improvisation and from improvisation came the body of the text. It was not until well after the first run of the play that the text was actually written down. Therefore the idea of it now being set in print, though exciting seems somehow contrary to the way in which it was created. The written word accounts for only a small part of what the play really is...but what else is new?

The performance style of *The Anger in Ernest and Ernestine* is based on our work in the clown tradition. An important aspect of this tradition is that there is no "fourth wall." Ernest and Ernestine acknowledge that the audience members are right there in the theatre with them, either with a simple look or by talking directly to them. The role of the audience ranges from confidante, admirer to provocateur and judge. It's easier for audience members to identify with Ernest and Ernestine and what they go through during the course of the play because they actually have a relationship with them.

There are no hard and fast rules for the actors to determine when to refer directly to the audience. These moments must be simple and natural. It is important that the performers discover for themselves the playfulness of this interaction, first during rehearsal then again during performance.

As Ernest and Ernestine gradually descend into their hurt and their fury, the shared moments with the audience become less frequent. As their innocence fades, so does their openness. The increase of tension during the final scenes moves the play from the comic into the tragic. The tragic tone is heightened by Ernest and Ernestine's loss of relationship with the audience.

The nature of the work is extremely physical. The purpose of the stage directions in the text is to help impart a flavour of this physicality. Actors must be free to develop their own characters and "comic business" which make up such a large part of the piece.

ACT ONE

I LOVE YOU BECAUSE

UNPACKING

BREAKFASTS

MONOLOGUES

POETRY

WAITING/ERNEST'S WAY HOME

SPRINGSTEEN

ACCIDENT

FACE TO FACE WITH THEIR PASSION

ACT TWO

RELAXING IN THE AFTERGLOW

DINNER/LASSIE IS A BITCH

MONOLOGUES

PACT

YOU HATE ME DON'T YOU

TO YOUR CORNERS

MONOLOGUES

GUNS/I HATE YOU BECAUSE

Act One

I LOVE YOU BECAUSE

Black. The first version of the song "So Many
Reasons" begins. Lights up on ERNESTINE
in a small alcove extreme SL. Lights up on
ERNEST *in a small alcove extreme SR. A*
male voice and a female voice begin to sing.

So many reasons to fall in love
So many reasons for the moon up above
So many reasons for you and I
We'll be together till we die.

So many reasons for wind to blow
So many reasons for the rivers to flow
All of these reasons are sweet mystery
Now that I love you and you love me.

> ERNEST *and* ERNESTINE *step out of their*
> *alcoves and walk DS toward each other.*

We will never fall apart
The way so many people do
We will always tell each other
I'm still in love with you.

Instrumental portion of the song continues under dialogue.

ERNESTINE   I love you Ernest.

ERNEST   I love you Ernestine.

ERNESTINE   I love you because you're in your own sweet little world.

ERNEST   I love you because you have pizzaz. Pizzaz for just walking down the street.

ERNESTINE   I love you because you make me feel like Juliet.

ERNEST   Who?

ERNESTINE   Juliet. Romeo and Juliet. From Literature.

ERNEST   Oh.

They awkwardly approach each other and attempt to dance together. Music out.

ERNESTINE   I love you because you make me want to blush and I don't know why.

ERNEST   I love you because you make me want to marry you.

ERNEST *swoons backwards surprised by his own words.*

ERNESTINE   I love you because I knew you'd say that.

Black. Music—"So Many Reasons"—instrumental version.

UNPACKING

---

*Music continues. Lights up on a tiny and
unusual basement apartment. SL there is a
weighted stair unit which is suspended
horizontally just below the level of the ceiling.
It descends whenever the characters walk
down it after entering the apartment or when
it is pulled down by hand when they go back
up to leave. In the wall underneath the stairs
is a door which leads to a small closet. SR of
this is a freestanding coatrack. USC is a
temperamental old furnace, the most
prominent presence in the apartment. The
pipes of the furnace extend across the ceiling
of the apartment out towards the audience. SR
of the furnace is a door which leads to the
bedroom. Along the SR wall is a kitchen
cupboard with shelves and a sink. DSL of the
furnace is a small table and two chairs. An
empty packing box is on the table.* ERNEST
and ERNESTINE *enter and come down the
stair unit which slowly swings down as they
make their descent. They both carry more
boxes,* ERNEST *carries a broom.*
ERNESTINE *takes a tissue box and places it
on the table then crosses to the
cupboard/shelves to put away books, bowls,
paper towels, etc.* ERNEST *takes the tissue
box from the table and puts it in his box.
Music out.*

ERNESTINE   I love our basement home Ernest.

ERNEST   It's like a dream Ernestine.

They rub noses and coo "widgy widgy woo."

ERNEST   It's so warm. Snug as a rug on a bug. Snug as two rugs on two bugs ahuggin'.

ERNESTINE   I can't believe I'm going to see you every day.

ERNEST   Everyday. Day after day. (*more cooing*) I'm going to put my hammer up here on the shelf sweetie.

ERNESTINE   (*joyfully resuming her unpacking*) Uh-huh.

ERNEST   And the new broom close by...

ERNESTINE   Uh-huh.

ERNEST   And the cereal right here in the bookshelf...and your teapot over... What's this?

ERNESTINE   Sweetie they're teabags.

ERNEST   Sweetie you should always take the teabags out of the teapot.

ERNESTINE   Oh sweetie, Aunt Mildred always said you're supposed to leave them in. That way the teapot gets a nice roasty flavour of tea over the years.

ERNEST   That's tannic acid. Tannic acid is really bad.

ERNESTINE   Oh?

ERNEST   You should always, always take the teabags out of the teapot. It's not good sweetie, it's bad.

ERNESTINE   Oh of course, sweetie. That Aunt Mildred!

ERNEST   So, I thought I'd put your teapot up here on the shelf.

ERNESTINE   I thought, sweetie, we should keep it in the cupboard.

ERNEST   In the cupboard?! Okay. (*more cooing*) We need more
             shelves. Your things would fit here and my things
             would fit here but together they don't fit.

             They both laugh nervously. ERNEST
             unwittingly puts the hammer back into the box
             he is holding. He then places the tissue box on
             the top shelf, turns and sees a package of
             cigarettes on the table.

ERNEST   What's that?

ERNESTINE   It's my cigarettes, sweetie.

ERNEST   You don't smoke them?

ERNESTINE   Well, I didn't bother to tell you Ernest because I
             smoke maybe one cigarette a year on very cold nights.

ERNEST   I guess you won't have to worry about that in this
             place. Boy oh boy, this furnace really chugs out the
             heat!

             ERNEST *takes off his jacket/sweater and*
             goes to hang it on the coatrack.

ERNESTINE   I'll just put them away for that one nice cold winter
             night sweetie.

             ERNESTINE *"hides" her cigarettes in the*
             cupboard then takes the tissue box from the
             shelf and puts it back on the table.

ERNEST   I'll just put this empty box in the closet sweetie.

ERNESTINE   Oh Ernest, I thought that we could put all the coats on
             the coatrack, and the sweaters in the sweater drawer.

ERNEST   What a good idea!

                *ERNESTINE takes the sweater/jacket
                towards the bedroom.*

ERNEST   Where are you going with my jacket?

ERNESTINE   This? This is a sweater.

ERNEST   What? No, no sweetie, that's my jacket.

ERNESTINE   Isn't that funny, I was sure it was a sweater.

ERNEST   This? (*taking his jacket/sweater*) No, it's my good
                jacket. I've had it ever since I was in Boycubs with
                Mr. Garlic.

                *ERNEST hangs his jacket/sweater on the
                coatrack and moves the tissue box back to the
                shelf. He turns and becomes transfixed,
                staring into space.*

ERNESTINE   (*crossing to USL of Ernest*)
                Ernest?—Ernest!—ERNEST!!!

ERNEST   What? (*both jumping*) Oh, I'm sorry sweetie, I forgot
                you were here. It's like a dream.

ERNESTINE   Ernest, what were you looking at?

ERNEST   Oh, I was thinking I could paint a window. This is my
                first basement home and I think I'll miss the windows,
                but I could paint one for myself...with the sun
                streaming in, the rain and the lightning, the leaves
                changing colours, antelope running free.

ERNESTINE   Oh Ernest, I was so lucky to meet a man like you!

ERNEST   Ah, me too sweetie.

ERNESTINE   Ernest, I have a little something for you, for us. Close your eyes—No peeking—Come sit down. (*running to the closet*)

ERNEST   (*sitting*) Can I open my eyes now?

ERNESTINE   Not yet sweetie. (*placing a gaudy artificial plant on the table*) Okay you can open your eyes now.

ERNEST   Golly. Boy oh boy, look at that.

ERNESTINE   Do you like it sweetie?

ERNEST   Yes, oh yes. It's so darn colourful.

ERNESTINE   I like it because it doesn't pretend to be anything that it's not.

ERNEST   No, look at that, it doesn't pretend. It just sits there. You don't have to water it.

ERNESTINE   No.—

ERNEST   Won't grow, won't ever change. Where're you gonna put it?

ERNESTINE   Are you sure you like it sweetie?

ERNEST   Yes, oh yes!

ERNESTINE   Well I thought maybe it could go right here. (*crossing to cupboard and putting the plant on the top shelf*)

ERNEST   Would you look at that!

ERNESTINE   What?

ERNEST   There must be, how many places are there in our basement home?

ERNESTINE   Well, I suppose…

ERNEST   2000. Over 2000! And you picked the perfect spot!

ERNESTINE   Oh!

ERNEST   Sweetie, you're an artist.

ERNESTINE   No Ernest, you're the artist.

ERNEST   Ernestine you have art in you.

> *Strange sounds erupt.* ERNESTINE *realizes it's the furnace.* ERNEST *stands transfixed, staring at the plant. As the sounds grow louder and more ominous the furnace begins to glow. Steam seeps from the furnace and its pipes.*

ERNESTINE   Ernest it's the furnace.

ERNEST   Hmmm?

ERNESTINE   It's the furnace Ernest. ERNEST!!

ERNEST   It's the furnace Ernestine. To your stations!

ERNESTINE   What do we do Ernest? What do we do?

ERNEST   (*grabbing the furnace manual hanging above the furnace*) We look at the book that the landlord left. We must follow the rules calmly, methodically, thoroughly, step by step.

ERNESTINE   Ernest we have to do something!

ERNEST   Step by step. First step; "Get the hammer." Get the hammer sweetie.

ERNESTINE *looks in the cupboard.*

ERNESTINE   There is no hammer.

ERNEST   Of courses there's a hammer, I put it right up here on the…where's my hammer?

ERNESTINE *kicks the furnace.*

ERNEST   No, No! Step two; "Get the ratchet."

ERNESTINE   What's a ratchet?

ERNEST   What's a ratchet?

ERNESTINE   What's a ratchet?

ERNEST   A ratchet is a ratchet.

ERNESTINE   Well what does a ratchet look like?

ERNEST   It looks like a ratchet.

ERNESTINE   Well good for it!

ERNEST   Don't good for it Ernestine, just get it! Calmly go and get the ratchet that looks like a ratchet!

ERNESTINE *pulls the widget on the furnace.*

ERNEST   No, not the widget!

ERNESTINE   What's a widget?

ERNEST   That's a widget!

ERNESTINE   How am I supposed to know what a widget is?

ERNEST   Don't pull the…

ERNESTINE   I don't know what the...

ERNEST   Dd—

ERNESTINE   I—

> *The commotion of the furnace subsides.*
> *Pause.*

ERNEST   Boy oh boy.

ERNESTINE   Whew wee.

ERNEST   I guess we fixed it.

ERNESTINE   Yeah we did Ernest.

ERNEST   Good thing we followed the rules.

ERNESTINE   Yeah, good thing we followed the rules and I pulled the widget.

ERNEST   Boy oh boy. (*coming towards each other and meeting DSC, looking out at audience*) These old beasts can be pretty temperamental. Pretty temperamental.

> *Black. Music—"So Many*
> *Reasons"—instrumental version.*

BREAKFASTS

BREAKFAST #1: *Lights up as music fades.*
ERNEST *is seated at the table about to have
breakfast. His bowl and milk are meticulously
arranged on the table. He is in the midst of
opening the cornflakes box. He catches sight
of audience and smiles. He lovingly pours his
cereal, neatly closes the box then pours the
milk, marvelling over every step of the ritual.
He is about to begin eating his cereal when*
ERNESTINE *enters, flustered. He grins at the
sight of her. She runs to* ERNEST, *mutters
"good morning sweetie," runs to the
cupboard, grabs two bowls, drops one and
puts it back in the cupboard. She runs to the
table, tears open the cereal box, pours and
spills the cereal then gathers loose flakes in
her skirt and dumps them in her bowl. She
pours the milk.* ERNEST *watches in
fascinated disbelief. She eats.*

ERNESTINE   Oh, no.

ERNESTINE *rushes into the bedroom and
returns with her hat and shoes. She throws
down the shoes and tries to put them on while
eating. She crawls under the table and runs
around the kitchen attempting to get her shoes
on. After spinning, jumping and dancing, her
shoes are on.*

ERNEST   Boy sweetie, you sure are spunky in the morning.

                ERNESTINE *gets lipstick from her purse and
                dabs it on her cheeks using milk to rub it in.
                She gets a banana from the cupboard, runs to
                the table, peels the banana, breaks it in two,
                throwing the pieces into the bowl. She runs
                back to the cupboard, throws the peel in the
                garbage and runs back to the table and eats.*

ERNESTINE   Oh!

                ERNESTINE *jumps up, goes into the
                bedroom and returns, brushing her teeth. She
                alternates between eating her cereal and
                brushing her teeth. She looks at her watch
                and leaps up. She puts her bowl away in the
                cupboard.*

ERNESTINE   Bye sweetie.

                ERNESTINE *exits up the stairs. Before*
                ERNEST *can catch his breath she reappears
                at the top of the stairs.*

ERNESTINE   ERNEST, MY HAT!

                ERNEST *jumps up, grabs her hat and tosses
                it to her.* ERNESTINE *exits.* ERNEST *stands
                dumbfounded, then smiles.*

ERNEST   Boy oh Boy.

                *Black. Music—"So Many
                Reasons"—instrumental version.*

                BREAKFAST #2: *Lights up as music fades.*
                ERNEST *is about to pour his milk. He
                flinches and looks toward the bedroom,
                thinking he hears* ERNESTINE. *He looks out*

at the audience, smiles and continues to pour his milk.

ERNESTINE (*enters muttering*) Morning sweetie.

> ERNESTINE *gets a bowl from the cupboard.* ERNEST *attempts to pour her cereal for her. She sits momentarily then jumps up to get her shoes, hat and purse from the bedroom. She sits back down then jumps up to get a banana, peels the banana, shoves half in her mouth, half in her purse. She runs around in tiny circles trying to get her shoes on. After spinning, dancing, jumping, they're on. She takes lipstick from her purse and puts it on her cheeks, taking milk from* ERNEST'S *bowl, dabbing it on her cheeks. She then eats a couple of spoonfuls of cereal out of his bowl.* ERNEST *tries to hide from the entire spectacle by reading the back of the cereal box, sometimes aloud.* ERNESTINE *exits up the stairs then returns.*

ERNESTINE ERNEST!

> ERNEST *tosses her hat a little more aggressively than the first time, looks out, and smiles, hesitantly.*

ERNEST Boy oh Boy.

> *Black. Music—Urban Rhythms—instrumental.*

> **BREAKFAST #3:** *Lights up as music fades.* ERNEST *sits gripping the cereal box tightly, hiding behind it. When* ERNESTINE *enters he scrunches the box.*

ERNESTINE (*mumbling*) Morning sweet.

ERNESTINE *grabs a handful of cereal, takes a slug of milk from the carton. It dribbles down her chin and on to her blouse. She goes to the cupboard, grabs a piece of paper towel and exits up the stairs unaware of the towel unrolling behind her. She returns and gasps.*

ERNESTINE   ER—.

ERNEST *throws* ERNESTINE'S *hat at her and she leaves.* ERNEST *re-rolls the paper towel then cleans up the kitchen, breathing quickly. When finished, he sighs, smiles, relaxes and rests his hand on the hot furnace. He grimaces, runs about the room flapping his hand and blowing on it in an attempt to ease the pain. He calms down and stands in silence. Suddenly he erupts with an angry scream. He looks sharply towards the stairway exit. Black. Music—Urban Rhythms—instrumental.*

MONOLOGUES

Music ends. Lights up on ERNESTINE *in SL alcove.*

ERNESTINE Meeting Ernest was like a dream. Marrying Ernest was also like a dream. Oh don't get me wrong, it's still like a dream. It's just a little bit funny how he just sits there in the morning reading the cereal. I would have thought that just one morning he would jump up and walk me to the Woolworth's hat department—that's where I work. Don't get me wrong I'm not complaining, Ernest is perfect. It just makes me feel a little bit funny how he just sits there...like he's in a coma or something.

Cross fade to ERNEST *in SR alcove.*

ERNEST Ernestine is like...she's like a little sparrow. A little bird flitting about the forest. Flapping her wings, making little windy sounds...flip-flap, flip-flap. Once I saw a Golden osprey, calmly winging its way across the deep blue sky. And this little sparrow rose up out of the forest and it started flitting all about the osprey, darting hither and thither. It darted underneath the osprey and it poked it in its belly, then it poked it on the head and it poked it in the eye and the osprey slowly turned over, took the little sparrow in its talons and squeezed its life out! I think I'll answer that help wanted ad I saw outside of Farley's Fish Shop. So maybe I can start really, really early in the morning, before Ernestine gets up. That way she can do...what she has to do.

Black. Ethereal instrumental music.

POETRY

Lights up. ERNESTINE *is seated at the table reading a poetry book, completely entranced.* ERNEST *is sitting in a chair DSR watching, perplexed, concerned. Black. Lights up.* ERNEST *is now sitting closer to the table, about 2 feet away. Black. Lights up.* ERNEST *is sitting at the table, staring at* ERNESTINE, *inches from her face. The music fades.*

ERNESTINE   Ernest, I could read this man's poetry every day and every night for the rest of my life. He's exquisite. I love him!

ERNEST screams, grabs the book out of ERNESTINE'S hands, rips it to shreds, stopping suddenly.

ERNEST   Ooopsie doodle. It's just that it's time to go shopping now. We're supposed to go shopping now. (*going to coatrack for his jacket/sweater*)

ERNESTINE   (*going to cupboard*) Where's the scotch-tape Ernest? We can fix it.

Black. Ethereal instrumental music.

WAITING/ERNEST'S WAY HOME

Lights up. Music fades.

ERNESTINE   It took me a while to convince Ursula Scarf, my boss, that I should have the whole day off. I wanted lots of time to get ready for my special time with Ernest. I wanted to go to dinner and then to a movie but as Ernest explained to me, it's best to go to the movie first because the early bird always gets the fresh popcorn.

ERNESTINE *smiles and notices the tissue box on the cupboard, places it on the table, sits and waits for* ERNEST *to arrive home. Cross fade to* ERNEST *in his alcove.*

ERNEST   I was hurrying out of Farley's Tropical Fish Shop, that's where I work, to begin the homeward path to my Ernestine and our special time together, when I beheld one of nature's horrible wonders—a mother guppie in the throes of birth. I knew exactly what to do, and with confident and trembling hands, I netted that mother guppie and placed her in the special mother guppie birthing tank. Now as horrible as it may sound, mother guppies have an insatiable and unforgivable desire to eat their babies, and as difficult as it may be, we must somehow come to grips with the dark and lasting truth that nature can sometimes be terrifying to perceive. And this is only one example, perhaps you can think of others. But in the face of such mystery, I could hardly breathe. Anticipating the sight of the new-born baby guppies on their free fall to safety I stood and waited...

Quick cross fade to ERNESTINE, *sitting in the apartment, waiting. She begins to get warm and fans herself with her scarf. She attempts to get her scarf off but the knot seems to be stuck. She struggles with it, almost choking herself. Finally she gets the scarf off and throws it to the ground in a great frenzy. Cross fade back to* ERNEST *in alcove.*

ERNEST And oh what a dazzling spectacle it was. Twenty-seven new-born baby guppies swimming free. And just as the twenty-eighth baby guppie was being wrenched from its mother's womb, Farley, the owner of Farley's Tropical Fish Shop, came and told me in no uncertain terms to "Get the hell out of the store Ernest!!" Now as unforgivable as the tone of Farley's voice may have been, he had thankfully brought me face to face with the fact that the special time with my Ernestine to which I had sacredly avowed myself was slipping away like sand on the beach of time. I leapt onto that homeward path and followed it rapidly...

Cross fade to ERNESTINE, *waiting. She gets more frustrated and impatient as the scene goes on. She looks expectantly at the top of the stairs. She opens her purse, takes out tissues, tosses them on the floor. She takes gum from her purse, chews it, snaps the purse shut. She opens her purse, takes a few tissues from the tissue box, juggles them, stuffs them in her purse and snaps it shut. She repeats this pattern one or two more times. She takes her hat and begins to play with it, twisting it into different shapes. She becomes rougher until the scene climaxes with* ERNESTINE *strangling the hat. Quick cross fade to* ERNEST'S *alcove.*

ERNEST I was hurrying along the homeward path that led me straight to my Ernestine and our special time together,

ERNEST   when I noticed a tiny object precariously perched above the letter T of the word STOP of the second homeward STOP sign. There, twittering in its confusion, was a Ruby-Crested Nuthatch that had inexplicably strayed at least 300 miles from its normal migratory flight path. I stood in silence, memorizing its characteristics and features so that I could later record them in my Boycub bird identification book that I'd been given as a gift from Mr. Garlic. I was sure that it was a Ruby-Crested Nuthatch...

> *Cross fade to* ERNESTINE *standing in the apartment leaning on the back of the chair.*

ERNESTINE Ernest and I have a very special relationship. Even when we're apart, we're together. That's why I don't feel abandoned right now. In fact I know that Ernest will be home very shortly. By the time I count to ten, Ernest will walk through the door. Watch.

> ERNESTINE *turns DS and brings the chair with her. Her hands are clamped to it. She prys her hands away from the chair and moves DS. She begins counting, with intermittent "loosening up exercises" to help her tune in to* ERNEST.

ERENSTINE One...two...three...four...five...six...seven...eight... nine...ten.

> *Black.* ERNESTINE *screams. Lights up on* ERNEST'S *alcove.*

ERNEST   Just as the moment of positive identification was upon me, my bird bolted desperately away. I wheeled around to see that it was a man with a dog that had scared away my bird, a man with a seeing-eye dog and he appeared to be blind—the man, not the dog. Anyway I was about to continue on that homeward

ERNEST path when I saw the man do this (*picking lint off his shirt, looking at it then flicking it away*). It was my feeling that this blind man was bluffing! And in order to report him to the proper authorities, I followed him to the dark side of town where he cruelly strapped his dog to a post outside a bar. Well I followed him into that bar, just to give him fair warning of my intent to report...and he turned out to be a swell fellow! Sharky. And Sharky said that this blind man's bluff was the only way he could keep his dog—his one true friend in the world. And to prove his love for that dog, he took it out a pitcher of beer. I stood in awe as I watched the two of them winding their way home through the traffic. And it was only then that I noticed that it was dark. So I leapt onto that homeward path and I rushed, I literally raced to be home with my Ernestine.

Lights up in the apartment, ERNESTINE *is sitting on the chair in a state of quiet desperation, laughing.* ERNEST *descends the stairs.*

ERNEST Hi sweetie, I'm home.

ERNESTINE walks DS. The lights change. She is not talking to ERNEST but telling the audience the thoughts that are going through her mind.

ERNESTINE Ernest arrived home. He was 6 hours, 17 minutes and 42 seconds late. I watched him coming towards me. I don't know why I've never noticed it before but Ernest looks like a fish. With his googly eyes and his googly glasses, his hands like little fins. Ernest doesn't walk, he swims. I felt like I was going to explode! This time, I'm going to let him have it. I'm going to let him know what it's like to be kept waiting for 6 hour 17 minutes and 42 seconds. I'm going to

ERNESTINE   pick him up and hurl him through that stupid, ugly
            painted window...

ERNEST   Sorry I'm late sweetie. Ernestine?

            The lights are restored and she faces
            ERNEST.

ERNESTINE   Ernest?

ERNEST   Sorry I'm late. I couldn't help it.

ERNESTINE   Oh that's okay sweetie, I understand.

ERNEST   It's probably too late to go to a movie and dinner but
            we could still go down to the all-night variety store
            and get a ginger ale or something.

ERNESTINE   That's a good idea sweetie.

ERNEST   Okay, let's go. (*cleaning up* ERNESTINE'S *mess of*
            tossed tissues and gum)

ERNESTINE   Sweetie.

ERNEST   Okay, let's go. (*still cleaning*)

ERNESTINE   Ernest, if we don't go right now we'll miss last call for
            ginger ale.

ERNEST   Okay, let's go. (*still cleaning*)

ERNESTINE   Ernest just do me one little favour.

ERNEST   What?

ERNESTINE   Don't wear that sweater.

ERNEST   What?

ERNESTINE I'd appreciate it if you didn't wear that stupid, ugly old sweater.

ERNEST   This is my good jacket.

Black. Ethereal music—instrumental.

SPRINGSTEEN

ERNEST *stands with a broom silhouetted in the furnace glow. The music fades. The lights come up in the rest of the apartment.* ERNEST *sweeps the floor. He goes to the cupboard and takes out a cassette tape and looks at it reverently. He puts it in the tape recorder and waits. Bruce Springsteen's "No Surrender" begins to play.* ERNEST *gets the feel of the music then gradually begins to lip sync the song. He gets more involved and starts performing rock star moves, dancing, using his broom as both a microphone and a guitar.* ERNESTINE *enters down the stairs and watches* ERNEST *with amusement.*

ERNESTINE Hi sweetie, I'm home.

ERNEST *immediately runs to the tape recorder, shuts it off and, greatly embarrassed, resumes sweeping.*

ERNESTINE What's that music Ernest? It's very pretty.

ERNEST Pretty? It's just an old tape.

ERNESTINE It's nice.

ERNEST It's not nice. It's just an old tape.

ERNESTINE Why don't you put the music on again, sweetie?

ERNESTINE *goes into the bedroom.*
ERNEST *puts the music back on. He becomes*

more involved with his fantasy and performs
for the audience as if he's performing for a
crowd of rock fans. ERNESTINE enters and
attempts to share his fun, dancing around.
ERNEST doesn't notice her. His moves
become so aggressive that ERNESTINE has
to move out of his way to avoid being run
over. The fantasy is no longer fun for
ERNESTINE and she tries to tell the
audience to stop encouraging ERNEST.
ERNEST finally sees ERNESTINE and
reacts by screaming and breaking the broom
over his knee. ERNESTINE runs over to the
recorder and slams it off.

ERNESTINE Ernest, you broke the broom!

ERNEST So!?

ERNESTINE Ernest, you broke the broom!!

ERNEST So, I broke the broom. So!?

ERNESTINE Ernest, you broke the broom!!

ERNESTINE storms into the bedroom and
slams the door behind her.

ERNEST I really did break the broom! I don't have anything
against brooms. I really like brooms. I just don't like it
when Ernestine's in my audience.

Black. Music—Urban Rhythms—instrumental.

ACCIDENT

Lights up as music ends. ERNEST *and*
ERNESTINE *enter the apartment via the*
stairs in emotional and physical disarray.

ERNEST   It was awful.

ERNESTINE   It was really awful Ernest! We came this close. Did
your life pass in front of you?

ERNEST   Just the ugly parts.

ERNESTINE   It was that brick. That brick was the final straw. It
came—kkkk...(*noise of crash*)

ERNEST   It shouldn't have been there. None of it. It was really,
really ugly.

ERNESTINE   Sit down Ernest.

ERNEST   Sit down Ernestine. I want you to calm down.

ERNESTINE   (*sitting at the table.*) If the highway department would
put up their signs like they're supposed to, we would
have known it was a one-way street, right? How were
we to know it was a one-way street, Ernest? How
were we to know?

ERNEST   There was an arrow pointing up. I saw an arrow
pointing up.

ERNESTINE   What's that supposed to mean?

ERNEST   It means they botched it Ernestine. All those people,
                coming out of their homes, yelling mean things at us.
                They botched it with that arrow sign Ernestine.

ERNESTINE   And that moving van coming down the wrong way,
                the right way...coming right at us. What choice did
                we have Ernest? What choice?!

ERNEST   No choice!!

ERNESTINE   I think it was a children's playground we went
                through. Didn't you see that fence we crashed
                through?

ERNEST   All I saw was a sign with the shadow of a child
                running free on a yellow triangle.

ERNESTINE   The highway department. It's just not fair. We could
                sue them Ernest.

ERNEST   A little child...with little stick legs...little round
                head...

ERNESTINE   In fact, I think that's what we should do.

                ERNESTINE *goes to the cupboard, takes out
                a pen and sheet of paper and returns to the
                table.*

ERNESTINE   We should write them a letter. (*writing*) Oh, this pen
                doesn't work.

ERNEST   Don't worry about the pen.

ERNESTINE   I want to write a letter. We have to write a letter! It
                was this close!

ERNEST   They have no right. It's ludicrous!

ERNESTINE   It's ludicrous what they do out there. The government is ludicrous.

ERNEST   We should write a letter. This pen doesn't work.

ERNESTINE   Don't worry about the pen, just write it.

ERNEST   To whom it may concern...

ERNESTINE   We were nearly killed.

ERNEST   To whom not "it may." To whom it does concern.

ERNESTINE   To whom it does concern!

ERNEST   And I am going to underline the does!

ERNESTINE   That's good Ernest. (*grabbing the pen and paper and writing*) Underline it three times and put an exclamation mark. We were nearly killed!

ERNEST   To whom it better concern! (*grabbing paper and pen back*)

ERNESTINE   Yeah! To whom it better concern. That's good Ernest.

ERNEST: To whom it damn well better concern!

ERNESTINE   Yeah Ernest! Yeah! Or else!

ERNEST   To whom it (*pausing*) to whom it damn well better concern, or else!!

ERNESTINE   Or fuckin' else, Ernest! Fuckin' else!!

ERNEST   Fuckin' else! To whom it damn well better concern or fuck you!!

ERNESTINE   That's good Ernest! Keep it!!! To whom it fuckin' better concern or fuck off!!!

ERNEST   To whom it...to whom it fuckin' better concern or fuck off...fuck you...

ERNESTINE   Fuck you!

ERNEST   Fuck...fuck off or fuck you?

ERNESTINE   Both!!!

ERNEST   Both. Both!! To whom it fuckin' better concern or both fuck off and fuck you!!!

ERNESTINE   That's good Ernest! That's good. Now what goes next? We were nearly killed...

ERNEST   No. Oh no! You nearly killed us!

ERNESTINE   You did!

ERNEST   You did!

ERNESTINE   You tried to kill us!

ERNEST   You did!

ERNESTINE   You...

ERNEST   You...

ERNESTINE   You...

ERNEST   You bastards!

ERNESTINE   Bastards, that's good Ernest!

ERNEST   Bastards!

ERNESTINE	Bastards!
ERNEST	Bastards!
ERNESTINE	Bastards! Just keep writing Ernest, we don't want to miss any of the details.
ERNEST	Bastards!
ERNESTINE	The bricks...
ERNEST	Bastards!
ERNESTINE	The kids, the fence, the yelling...
ERNEST	You bastards fuck off!!
ERNESTINE	That's good, keep it!!!
ERNEST	(*standing*) You bastards can fuck right off!!!
ERNESTINE	(*standing*) Can fuck right off! You fuckin' bastards can fuckin' fuck right the fuck off!!!
	(*They sit and read to themselves what they have written.*)
ERNESTINE	Too many fuckin's? (*pausing*) Ernest, we only have one life to live and they nearly took it away! Write that down.
ERNEST	I will.
ERNESTINE	No. No. (*standing grabbing the letter and putting it in her purse*) I'm going to tell them. I'm going to go right out there and...
ERNEST	No, don't go out there.

ERNESTINE   I'm going out there because we're sitting here like
             dodos on a log...

ERNEST   You can't go out there.

ERNESTINE   Ernest, I'm not going to sit here like a dodo on a log.

             *They collide in front of the table, pushing and
             shoving like children.*

ERNESTINE   I'm—

ERNEST   You can't—

ERNESTINE   Dodo—

ERNEST   Don't go—

ERNESTINE   I'm not—(*gasping, clapping her hand over her mouth
             and backing away*) Oh Ernest!

ERNEST   What?

ERNESTINE   Your face.

ERNEST   My face?

ERNESTINE   Your face is a bit squished in. The fence it...You have
             the imprint of the fence on your face.

ERNEST   (*turning his back to the audience*) Does it look funny?
             Do I look funny?

ERNESTINE   I still love you Ernest.

ERNEST   They had no right to put a fence there!

ERNESTINE   Well then you go out there and tell them.

ERNEST	You think I look ugly.
ERNESTINE	You don't look ugly, you just have a face that's a bit squished in.
ERNEST	I have a face that looks like a fence!
ERNESTINE	(*pausing*) Ernest, we could sue them!
ERNEST	Those bastards!

They turn and glare at the audience. Black.

FACE TO FACE WITH THEIR PASSION

> *Black. The roar of the furnace is heard. Lights up. The apartment is dimly lit. The furnace glows.* ERNEST *is sitting in front of the furnace, holding the manual, looking perplexed.* ERNESTINE *enters through the bedroom door, overheated and agonized.*

ERNESTINE Still no luck, sweetie? Sweetie? I don't believe it! Ernest. ERNEST!

ERNEST What?! What are you doing to me?

ERNESTINE I'm not doing anything to you. I simply came into this inferno to find out if you've had any luck.

ERNEST You yelled.

ERNESTINE No I did not yell.

ERNEST You yelled at me!

ERNESTINE Oh, Ernest. Did it sound like I was yelling?

ERNEST Yes it did. Remarkably so.

ERNESTINE I'm sorry, sweetie. It's just that I can't quite believe that you still haven't figured out how to turn off the furnace.

ERNEST It remains a grave mystery to me, sweetie.

ERNESTINE Have you tried pulling the widget?

ERNEST   The widget has nothing to do with it.

ERNESTINE   I think you should try pulling the widget again.

ERNEST   Leave the widget completely out of it. The widget is a
                  blind alley leading nowhere!

ERNESTINE   We have to do something, Ernest. This heat is
                  unbearable. (*slowly sinking to the floor*) I'm melting,
                  Ernest. I'm melting away to nothing. What are we
                  going to do Ernest?

ERNEST   We are going to remain calm and look at the book that
                  the landlord left.

ERNESTINE   (*getting up*) Why look at that stupid book? That book
                  is stupid!

ERNEST   Ernestine, the book that the landlord left is not stupid!

ERNESTINE   Fine. Then suppose you tell me, if the book is not
                  stupid Ernest, then what is it?

ERNEST   What is what?

ERNESTINE   The book Ernest. What is the book?

ERNEST   The book is a step by step manual of maintenance for
                  a temperamental heating device.

ERNESTINE   Then why doesn't it tell us how to turn it off?

ERNEST   That remains a major part of the mystery.

ERNESTINE   Fine, it's not a stupid book; it's a mystery book.
                  Maybe it's a Gothic novel. Just what are we going to
                  do?

ERNEST   We are going to endure a difficult situation, and I
                suggest we do it without yelling.

ERNESTINE   What about melting Ernest? How are we going to
                endure it without melting?

ERNEST   Ernestine, I do not enjoy melting any more than you
                do, but what about the people who take their holidays
                down at Disney World?! Can't you, just for a moment,
                try to think about them?

                        ERNEST *turns to study the furnace.*
                        ERNESTINE *attempts to figure out*
                        ERNEST'S *logic but can't. She whimpers*
                        quietly.

ERNEST   What's wrong with you?

ERNESTINE   Ernest, why should I think about the poor people
                who take their holidays down at Disney World?

ERNEST   Sweetie, Disney World is in Florida!

ERNESTINE   I know that Disney World is in Florida. What I want to
                know is how my thinking about the poor people who
                take their holidays down there is going to make me
                feel any better about melting away in a basement
                apartment with a man with a book, with a furnace that
                won't turn off!

ERNEST   We have been prepared, Ernestine. All winter long this
                furnace has been bellowing out the heat, and now,
                here we are in the middle of summer and yes, the heat
                may seem hotter now, it may even be hotter now, but
                we have been prepared...

                        ERNEST *has loosened his tie and is trying to*
                        get his shirt off.

ERNESTINE   Ernest, what are you trying to say?

ERNEST   Think about those northern Canadian school children! Year after year they're dragged out of their chilly northern homes, down, down to the Florida sunshine!

ERNESTINE   Ernest, for God's sake what are you saying?

ERNEST   I can't get my shirt off. I'm trapped! My sweltering body is trapped in a tropical hell.

ERNESTINE *tries to help him.*

ERNEST   The buttons are locked.

ERNESTINE   Come here, Ernest. Stop it.

ERNEST   What are you doing? You're doing something to me again, Ernestine!

ERNESTINE   I'm trying to help you.

ERNEST   Get away from me! Get AWAY!!!

ERNEST *pushes* ERNESTINE *away. She falls to the floor. He tears open his shirt, rips it off and hurls it to the floor. Pause.*

ERNESTINE   Oh, Ernest!

ERNEST   Hello Ernestine.

ERNESTINE   Hi Ernest.

ERNEST *steps toward* ERNESTINE. *The "rock" version of "So Many Reasons" begins to play.* ERNEST *gracefully pulls* ERNESTINE *to her feet...They caress each others' arms and tingle in reaction. She places her first hand on his left hip, the second on his right hip and then pulls him closer. The scene continues with a series of gymnastic, erotic and humorous positions spaced by blackouts.*

End of Act One

Act Two

RELAXING IN THE AFTERGLOW

The furnace glows and emits steam.
Music—"So Many Reasons"—"Smoke"
version. ERNEST *enters from the closet on all*
fours, exhausted. He heads for the bedroom. A
small bark is heard from the closet. ERNEST
"woofs" like a large dog. ERNESTINE
comes out of the closet barking like a frisky
puppy. They face each other on all fours and
have a playful conversation in animal sounds:
sheep, bulls, lions, birds, orangutans. As the
music sways into a sultry guitar solo, they
begin to dance. ERNEST *eventually lifts*
ERNESTINE *onto the table. He climbs on top*
and raises his arms in triumph. ERNESTINE
bites his ear. Music fades.

ERNESTINE Ernest, I don't ever want to stop.

ERNEST *growls.*

ERNESTINE Don't stop. Let's do it on the table. On the table,
Ernest. *(biting harder)*

ERNEST Ow...OW!

ERNESTINE   Oh Ernest you've awakened something in me, I don't want to stop! I've always wanted to do it on the table.

ERNEST   Ow...stop. On the table? (*disengaging*)

ERNESTINE   On the table, Ernest. Just let go...

ERNEST   On the table?

ERNESTINE   We can't stop now, sweetie...

ERNEST   On the table?! This is where I eat my breakfast! On the table?

> ERNESTINE *sits up awkward and vulnerable.* ERNEST *disengages completely. Pause.*

ERNESTINE   I got confused. I thought we were in the bedroom.

ERNEST   You said you always wanted to do it on the table.

ERNESTINE   I said, let's keep doing it if we're able. Let's just go to the bedroom.

ERNEST   You go to the bedroom. I'm going to go get something to eat. I haven't eaten for three days.

ERNESTINE   I'll come with you.

ERNEST   Uh...alright.

ERNESTINE   I'll just go freshen up.

> ERNEST *puts on his shirt and tie as* ERNESTINE *goes into the bedroom. She returns with her clothes and puts them on.*

ERNEST	We could go to that new Chinese restaurant up on the hill.
ERNESTINE	Anywhere you want, sweetie, but not Chinese food. I don't feel like it somehow.
ERNEST	Me neither. I know, let's go have a chicken dinner at the Chicken Ranch.
ERNESTINE	No, no. Not chicken, Ernest. We always have chicken. There must be something other than chicken, Ernest. Anywhere you want, sweetie, just use your imagination.
ERNEST	Hey! Let's go to Bingo's.
ERNESTINE	The Pizza Parlour? We should go somewhere a little bit different, don't you think?
ERNEST	What's wrong with pizza?
ERNESTINE	I don't like it anymore. (*taking the tissue box from the shelf*)
ERNEST	You never told me that.
ERNESTINE	It just slipped my mind, Ernest. I forgot to tell you.
ERNEST	What else have you forgotten to tell me?
ERNESTINE	Ernest, just decide where we're going to go for dinner. (*putting the tissue box back on the table*)
ERNEST	I have decided. We're going to Bingo's. You can eat my crusts.
ERNESTINE	Fine, we'll go to Bingo's.
ERNEST	I don't want to go to Bingo's.

ERNESTINE   Just where do you want to go for dinner, Ernest?

ERNEST   I want to go to RJ's.

ERNESTINE   Fine. We'll go to RJ's. Anywhere. I'm hungry. We'll
             go have chicken. I'll have Chinese chicken at the
             Pizza Parlour. Let's just go.

ERNEST   Are you okay?

ERNESTINE   I'm fine.

ERNEST   Are you sure?

ERNESTINE   I'm fine. Are you okay?

ERNEST   I'm fine. (*taking the tissue box from the table and
             putting it back on the shelf*) Let's go. Do you want to
             hear a joke?

ERNESTINE   Sure.

ERNEST   It's a good one. I saw it at RJ's last week. It's a
             graffiti. It said: "Lassie is a Bitch." Ha, ha. It's a good
             one.

ERNESTINE   I don't find that very funny. (*getting the tissue box*)

ERNEST   What? "Lassie is a Bitch"? It's a joke, sweetie.

ERNESTINE   (*placing tissue box on the table*) I realize it's a bit of a
             pun, but I don't find it very funny, it's anti-women.

ERNEST   Women have got nothing to do with it. It's a joke
             about a dog, sweetie. Lassie is a bitch, it's true, that's
             what she is.

ERNESTINE   Yes, but women have been called bitches for centuries.

ERNEST | So have female dogs. Cause that's what they are. They're bitches.

ERNESTINE | That's why it's unpleasant, to be referred to as a bitch.

ERNEST | It's not you that's the bitch, it's Lassie, the dog.

ERNESTINE | I realize that Lassie is a dog, Lassie come home, Lassie, but it wouldn't be considered funny if men didn't call women...

ERNEST | Oh, come on. The joke is very simple. Lassie is a bitch...bitch!

Pause.

ERNESTINE | Ernest, you just called me a bitch.

ERNEST | I don't believe this.

ERNESTINE | You just said...

ERNEST | What I said was...

ERNESTINE | It's very clear to me what you just said...

ERNEST | What I just said, if you'll listen, is Lassie is a bitch...bitch, emphasizing the word bitch. If I'd wanted to insult you, I would have said it a little differently.

ERNESTINE | And how would that have been?

ERNEST | Oh, I don't know. Maybe I would have said something like; Lassie is a bitch, BITCH!! But that's not what I said.

ERNESTINE | Ernest, if you want to call me a bitch, don't feel like you have to hide behind your stupid, silly little jokes.

ERNEST   I don't want to call you a bitch.

ERNESTINE   Do what you want, Ernest, come on, if you need...

ERNEST   I do not need that...

ERNESTINE   Come on Ernest, are you afraid? What's the matter?

ERNEST   No, I am not afraid...

ERNESTINE   What's wrong Ernest, are you...are you...?

ERNEST   I do not want...

ERNESTINE   WIMP!

ERNEST   COW!

ERNESTINE   Pig!

ERNEST   Slut!

ERNESTINE   Bastard!!

ERNEST   You're like some animal, you can't get it enough!

ERNESTINE   That's because you don't give it enough!

ERNEST   How can I with you drooling and howling in my ear
               like a bitch in heat!

ERNESTINE   Fuck Right Off!!!

ERNEST   You fuck off!

ERNESTINE   Just fuck off, Ernest!!

ERNEST   Fuck Off!

ERNESTINE   Fuck off!

ERNESTINE   Fuck off!

>   *They continue yelling "Fuck off."*
>   ERNESTINE *stops.* ERNEST *continues, the*
>   *words coming out in a high-pitched wail. He*
>   *stops.*

ERNESTINE   Ernest, I'm sorry.

>   *Black.*

MONOLOGUES

Lights up on ERNESTINE *in SL alcove.*

ERNESTINE I'd just like to take this opportunity to apologize to you. What you've been seeing isn't really me. I don't know who it is you've been seeing, but it isn't me. Like the other day, the other day in the supermarket, this sweet little woman came up to me and asked me where the teabags were kept. And I said: "In the teapot, Goddamn it, in the Goddamn teapot!!!" And I really enjoyed saying it. But it wasn't me who was enjoying it. It wasn't me. And Ernest isn't being Ernest. But I'm sure there's a way of finding ourselves again, there must be! But until then, I've made a short, little list of words that Ernest should avoid using in my presence: teabags, tissue box, table, Lassie...

Lights fade on ERNESTINE *and up on* ERNEST *in his alcove.*

ERNEST I read about marriage...in the pamphlets at the back of the church...it was there I think I read the words "You always hurt the one you love." Or maybe it was a poem. It doesn't matter where. The important thing is I've been thinking about the words "You always hurt the one you love" and I've begun to wonder to myself from time to time, who exactly is the "you"? Who is hurting who? I know that Ernestine hurts me from time to time, unintentionally of course, and I know that I would never do a thing to hurt my Ernestine, but who is the "you" who is always hurting the one you love? (*beginning to sing*) "You always hurt the one you..." It's a song! They shouldn't be singing jolly

ERNEST   little tunes about that! It's true! People should be prepared for things like that. Urgent messages should be sent out on a daily basis! "You always hurt the one you love. Be prepared!" Ernestine and I are. We have prepared ourselves with a powerful and intricate pact.

PACT

> ERNESTINE *and* ERNEST *leave their alcoves and walk toward each other, pretending to fume.*

ERNESTINE Grr...oh, grrrrr!

ERNEST Grrrrr.

ERNESTINE Pshshsh...

ERNEST What's that?

ERNESTINE Steam.

ERNEST Oh, pshshshsh...grrrr...Okay, now?

ERNESTINE Okay...

ERNEST Ernestine, look at the judge.

> *They wink at each other and go to opposite ends of the stage.* ERNEST *does push-ups,* ERNESTINE *does Tai Chi.*

ERNESTINE (*repeating*) Monkey picking peaches.

> *They come together, inhale, raising their arms and exhale bringing their arms down. They link arms facing the audience.*

ERNEST Do you, Ernestine, take this man to be your husband?

ERNESTINE   I do. Do you Ernest take this woman to be your wife?

ERNEST   I sure do.

ERNESTINE   That's just how he said it too!

ERNEST   It's true.

They kiss.

ERNESTINE   Oh, this is going to work like a charm!

ERNEST   It's those push-ups, when I do them the anger just flows out my arms, gone.

ERNESTINE   Ernest, I think that we should just explain. Ernest and I have decided that whenever we're really steamed up, when we feel like we're going to explode right through the roof, Ernest is going to call out "Look at the judge," and then we'll run to our corners and...

ERNEST   Yeah, but, you could say it too, sweetie. Either one of us could say it.

ERNESTINE   But, remember, it was always going to be you who called out "Look at the judge," and then we'd go running to our spots...

ERNEST   No I don't remember that, 'cause I might not be able to say it. It could be either one of us.

ERNESTINE   Ernest, remember? I suggested it and you agreed that we should keep the system simple and that it would always be you who'd say "Look at the judge," remember?

ERNEST   No, sweetie, I don't remember that it would always be me because what if I can't do it?

ERNESTINE   Ernest, don't get amnesia now.

ERNEST   I do not have amnesia. Just, what if I'm trapped, what if I'm locked and I can't say it? You should have as much responsibility as I.

ERNESTINE   Ernest, you're being childish. You are—

ERNEST   I am not being childish. I just might not be able to say it. I could get...

ERNESTINE   Ernest, it's the one rule I've made up in this apartment.

ERNEST   Ernestine!

ERNESTINE   What?

ERNEST   You cannot make up rules!

ERNESTINE   You make up rules all the time.

ERNEST   I most certainly do not.

ERNESTINE   Ernest!

ERNEST   Listen, Ernestine, there is a natural existing order to things, and if you interpret that order correctly, you have a rule.

ERNESTINE   Ernest, this isn't a Boycub field trip with Mr. Garlic, we're talking peace here, between you and me.

ERNEST   I am talking peace, and you have as much responsibility for keeping peace as I do.

ERNESTINE   Oh, Ernest, you're doing this to provoke me, you're always...

ERNEST   I am not, I just think you...

ERNESTINE   Ernest, stop it, you...

ERNEST   Awwwh, look at the fucking judge!!

ERNESTINE   See!!

ERNEST   Shut up and do your fucking monkey business!

ERNESTINE   It's Tai Chi!!!

They do the ritual, both furious.

ERNEST   Do you Ernestine take this man to be your husband?

ERNESTINE   I do. Do you Ernest take this woman to be your wife?

ERNEST   Sure I do.

ERNESTINE   That's not how you said it...*(turning, waiting for*
             ERNEST *to complete the ritual by kissing her)* We
             kiss now. Ernest you have to kiss me.

ERNEST   I can't kiss you.

             ERNESTINE *is shocked. She stands still for a*
             moment, then slowly collects her hat and
             purse and exits up the stairs. ERNEST *takes a*
             moment to realize what has happened. He
             then rushes to the stairs.

ERNEST   ERNESTINE!!

             ERNESTINE *appears at the top of the stairs.*

ERNESTINE   Ernest!

ERNEST   Look at the judge!!!

             They do the ritual rushing through it
             desperately. After the kiss they attempt to

*collect themselves by sitting together at the
table. There is a long moment of silence. They
are dazed and exhausted. ERNEST slowly
rises, begins to clean up the apartment. He
stops. Black. Music—Urban
Rhythms—instrumental.*

YOU HATE ME DON'T YOU

Lights up on the apartment. Music continues.
ERNEST *enters from the bedroom and tears*
around the apartment, looking for something.
He furiously empties the cupboard, shelves
and closet. ERNESTINE *enters down the*
stairs. Pause.

ERNEST   You hate me, don't you?

ERNESTINE   What?

ERNEST   You hate me, don't you? Don't you?!

ERNESTINE   Ernest, what's wrong?

ERNEST   I'll tell you what's wrong. You threw away my jacket!
You left the teabags in the teapot, you left the tissue
box on the table, and my hammer is missing!! Why do
you hate me?

ERNESTINE   Ernest, calm down.

ERNEST   I don't want to calm down.

ERNESTINE   Ernest, let's just sit down.

ERNEST   I don't want to let's just sit down, I want to know why
you hate me.

ERNESTINE   Ernest, I'm sorry if you can't find your sweater.

ERNEST   It's a jacket!!!

ERNESTINE   Ernest...

ERNEST   It's a Goddamn jacket!!!

ERNESTINE   Ernest, would you just let me say that I wouldn't dream of touching that smelly old sweater...

ERNEST   It's not a sweater, it's a jacket!!!

ERNESTINE   And I've never seen that hammer, I don't believe it exists!

ERNEST   It exists!

ERNESTINE   And the teabags should stay in the teapot, and the tissue box looks better right here!

        ERNEST *steps towards* ERNESTINE.

ERNESTINE   Stay where you are, don't come near me!

ERNEST   Don't worry, Ernestine, I wouldn't dream of coming near you. In fact, I'm not even going to look at you until you apologize to me!!!

        Long pause.

ERNESTINE   Ernest, you're right. I should apologize. Will you forgive me? It's just that I feel so inadequate next to you. That was terrible how I came home in such a mousey way. It's just so hard to measure up to your dramatics. Can I do it again, sweetie? This time I promise I'll be more like Liz Taylor. Oh, Ernest, let's make a movie of it! That'll be fun. We'll put the cameras out there, and the lights over by the tissue box. Oh, you'll love this Ernest, because you'll get to

ERNESTINE   say, "you hate me, don't you? Don't you?", just like you did before. It's so exciting being greeted like that!

ERNEST   Ernestine...

ERNESTINE   Quiet on the set!! We'll call the movie "King Tut Ernest, and his 210 Commandments."

ERNEST   Ernestine?

ERNESTINE   QUIET ON THE SET!!! Lights, camera, action. King Tut Ernest, alone on his mountaintop, looks down on his empire and feels sad because one of his subjects disobeyed his rule about leaving the teabags in the teapot. Just then, his most pathetic wife, Queen Ernestine, enters his chamber. I'm going to have to rehearse this a little bit sweetie, I'm just a stupid wife, not a great actor like you. I look up at you, feeling sick, sick with guilt, because it was me, I admit it, it was me who left the teabags in the teapot! I crawl to you—no, no, no, no, no crawling is too good for me, I slither to you on my belly, like the worm that I really am—if I could get any lower, Ernest, I would—I clutch at your long, white jacket/robe, which I shamefully mistook to be a sweater. I pull myself up, looking at perfection itself, I throw myself into your arms, begging for forgiveness. What do you want me to do now, King Tut Ernest? I'll do anything, anything. What do you want me to do now?!

ERNEST   Stop it Ernestine, you're like a crazy woman!!!

TO YOUR CORNERS

> *Ethereal Music.* ERNEST *and* ERNESTINE
> *retreat to their alcoves, eventually they*
> *approach each other.*

ERNESTINE   Ernest, just let me—

ERNEST   No, Ernestine, I want—

ERNESTINE   Ernest, shh I just—

ERNEST   Ernestine, no, shh...

ERNESTINE   shhh!!

ERNEST   shhh!!

ERNESTINE   zzzt—

ERNEST   ugh—

ERNESTINE   ooo—

ERNEST   tts—

ERNESTINE   a—

ERNEST   a—

ERNESTINE   ttszt—

They return to their alcoves, their bodies
wrenched and contracted. They recover and
approach each other.

ERNESTINE   Ernest, it's nobody's fault here.

ERNEST   I know.

ERNESTINE   It's not my fault, it's not your fault...

ERNEST   What are you looking over there for?

ERNESTINE   Don't be silly, Ernest, I said it's nobody's fault. It's not my fault, it's not your fault...

ERNEST   Why don't you look at me when you say that?

ERNESTINE   Oh, Ernest, don't, I said...

ERNEST   What are you really saying?

ERNESTINE   Ernest, you're being childish.

ERNEST   I am not being childish, it's just, what are you really saying?

ERNESTINE   Alright, Ernest, it is your fault! That's what you wanted me to say, and it's true!

ERNEST   It's all my fault!!!

ERNESTINE   It's all your fault!!!

They continue shouting this as they return to
their alcoves and attempt to get calm once
more. They try again.

ERNESTINE   Ernest, I think I know why this is all happening.

ERNEST   Suppose you tell me why Ernestine.

ERNESTINE   The problem is...it's because I...it's because—

ERNEST   What?!

ERNESTINE   It's because I feel judged by you.

ERNEST   Well that is a problem, because I know for a fact I
                 don't judge you.

ERNESTINE   Yes, but I feel judged.

ERNEST   But I do not judge you.

ERNESTINE   I don't know, Ernest, something you do...

ERNEST   Listen, I just said that I don't judge you.

ERNESTINE   But, Ernest, I feel judged.

ERNEST   Well then your feelings are false; because I don't.

ERNESTINE   Are you calling me a liar? That I don't know my own
                 feelings?

ERNEST   No, I'm just saying you're feeling falsely because...

ERNESTINE   They're my feelings Ernest!

ERNEST   What about my feelings?

ERNESTINE   You don't have any!!! (*hitting Ernest three times*)

> ERNEST *comes at her, chasing her toward
> the furnace.* ERNEST *turns and hits the
> furnace with all his force. Pause.*

ERNEST   I really hurt my hand, Ernestine.

They both begin to cry.

ERNESTINE   You shouldn't have hit the furnace, Ernest.

ERNEST   It really, really hurts.

ERNESTINE   I'm sorry, Ernest.

ERNEST   I'm sorry.

They continue to softly say "I'm sorry" as they both walk to their alcoves. Black.

MONOLOGUES

Lights up on ERNEST *and* ERNESTINE *in
their alcoves. They address their monologues
to each other rather than to the audience.*

ERNESTINE   I had this dream the other night, about you, Ernest. I
dreamt that your ears fell off. And I said to you,
"Ernest, put your ears back on," and you said, "What's
that, Ernestine? I can't hear you, my ears fell off."
And I said, "Ernest, put your ears back on," and you
said, "What's that Ernestine? I can't hear you, my ears
fell off." So I finally gave up and put your ears in my
purse. And I woke up feeling very, very tired.

ERNEST   I always thought that there was a natural existing
order to things, and if you interpreted that order
correctly you had a rule. But Ernestine, you make up
rules all the time. I guess that does something to the
old "natural existing order." So now I keep seeing
rules everywhere I go. At RJ's, I saw a rule, it was a
good one. It said, "If it feels good, do it!" But what if
it doesn't feel good? What if it feels really bad? Well,
I made up a rule, my first one…"If it feels bad, kill
it." It's a good rule.

*They each slowly raise an arm pointing a gun
at the other. The guns seem to have come from
nowhere.*

GUNS/I HATE YOU BECAUSE

Pause. They approach each other, slowly.

ERNESTINE I hate you Ernest.

ERNEST I hate you Ernestine.

Pause.

ERNESTINE I hate you because you never let me in...into your own stupid little world.

ERNEST I hate you because you never stop. Moving, turning, changing. (*pausing*)I hate you because I hate not knowing what to say to you.

ERNESTINE I hate you because I'm afraid to say things to you.

ERNEST I hate you because you say things that aren't true.

ERNESTINE I hate you because of the things you don't say.

ERNEST Like what?

ERNESTINE I can fix the furnace, Ernest. Why can't you say that?

ERNEST I hate you because you didn't follow the rules.

ERNESTINE I fixed the furnace!

ERNEST You fixed the furnace and you didn't even know what you were doing. (*pausing*)

ERNESTINE   I hate it because you can't admit that I'm right.

ERNEST   I hate it because I'm stupid and now you know it.

ERNESTINE   Ernest, I'm the one who's stupid.

ERNEST   Right.

Pause.

ERNEST   Wrong. You're not stupid.

ERNESTINE   Then why do you make me feel stupid?

ERNEST   Because I'm afraid of you.

ERNESTINE   What?

ERNEST   I'm afraid.

ERNESTINE   So am I.

They approach each other. Music—"So Many Reasons"—Finale. The guns are alternately dangerous and harmless as they begin to touch each other. They dance.

ERNESTINE   Where's your hat? I love that hat.

ERNEST puts his gun on the table and goes to get his hat. When he returns, wearing his hat, ERNESTINE hands him one of the guns she is holding. There is a moment of confusion about which gun is whose. Their eyes meet. Guns in hand, they dance gracefully about the apartment. They stand in an embrace as the lights and music fade.

The End